French

phr_____k

for kids

AA

About this book

Jane Wightwick
had the idea

Wina Gunn
wrote the pages

Leila & Zeinah Gaafar
(aged 10 and 12) drew the
first pictures in each
chapter

Robert Bowers
(aged 52) drew the other
pictures, and designed
the book

2

Important things that **must** be included

Marie-Claude Dunleavy did the French stuff (with some help from Alix Fontaine)

© g-and-w Publishing 2008

All rights reserved. No part of this publication may be reproduced, stored in a retrieval system, or transmitted in any form or by any means -- electronic, photocopying, recording or otherwise – unless the written permission of the publishers has been obtained beforehand. This book may not be sold, resold, hired out or otherwise disposed of by way of trade in any form of binding or cover other than that in which it is published, without the prior consent of the publisher.

A CIP catalogue record for this book is available from the British Library

ISBN: 978-0-7495-5950-2

Published by AA Publishing, a trading name of Automobile Association Developments Limited, whose registered office is Fanum House, Basing View, Basingstoke, Hampshire RG21 4EA. Registered number 1878835.

Colour separation by Keenes, Andover, UK

Printed and bound in China by Everbest

A03593

What's inside

Making friends

How to be cool with the group 6

Wanna play?

Our guide to joining in everything from hide-and-seek to the latest electronic game 30

Feeling hungry

Order your favourite foods or go local 52

Looking good

Make sure you keep up with all those essential fashions 62

Hanging out

At the pool, beach, or theme park—don't miss out on the action 70

Pocket money

Spend it here! 90

Grown-up talk

blah! blah! blah! blah!

If you really, really have to! 100

Extra stuff

All the handy things—numbers, months, time, days of the week 108

my big brother
mon grand frère
mo gro frair
grandpa
papi
pah-pee
grandma
mamie
ma-mee
dad
papa
pah-pah
mum
maman
ma-mon
my little sister
ma petite sœur
ma pteet sir

Half a step this way

stepfather/stepmother
beau–père/belle–mère
👄 bow pair/bel mair

stepbrother/stepsister
beau–frère/belle–sœur
👄 bow frair/bel sir

half brother/half sister
demi frère/demi sœur
👄 dumee frair/dumee sir

Hi! Salut!
👄 saloo

What's your name?
Comment tu t'appelles?
👄 ko–mo too tapel

My name's ...
Je m'appelle ...
👄 juh mapel

8

Kissing is extremely popular among French children. You can't possibly say hello to your friends in the morning without kissing them on both cheeks. Try this in front of your mirror if your friends at home won't let you experiment on them.

9

from Canada
du Canada
👄 doo kana-da

from Ireland
d'Irlande
👄 deer-lond

from Scotland
d'Écosse
👄 day-cos

from Wales
du Pays de Galles
👄 doo pay-ee duh gal

from the U.S.
des États-Unis
👄 days etaz-oo-nee

from England
d'Angleterre
👄 donglutair

Les textos

TOK? RAF...
TLM OQP 06.
koi29? @+.
2m1? biz x

Bet you're thinking – those letters and numbers in the French texts don't make sense! But remember: a French 1 is pronounced 'uh' (*un*), 2 is 'duh' (*deux*), and 9 is 'nuf' (*neuf*). The letter 'T' is pronounced 'tay' and 'P' is pronounced 'pay'. Get it now? … MDR!

TOK? (*t'es OK?*)
RUOK?

koi29? (*quoi de neuf?*)
WU? (*what's up?*)

MDR (*mort de rire*)
LOL (*laugh out loud*)

TLM (*tout le monde*)
EVRY1 (*everyone*)

OQP (*occupé*)
bizy

@+ (*a plus*)
CU L8R

STP (*s'il te plaît*)
PLZ

RAF (*rien a faire*)
nufN2do (*nothing to do*)

2m1 (*demain*)
2moro

biz (*bisous*)
luv

06 (*aussi*)
2 (*too*)

How old are you?
T'as quel âge?
👄 ta kel azh

12 years old
Douze ans
👄 dooz on

Happy birthday!
Bon anniversaire!
👄 bon anee-versair

What's your star sign?
C'est quoi, ton signe astrologique?
👄 say kwa toh seen-yastrolojeek

When's your birthday?
C'est quand, ton anniversaire?
👄 say kon, ton anee-versair

Star signs

AQUARIUS

Jan. 21 – Feb. 19
le Verseau 🗣 luhver-so

PISCES

Feb. 20 – Mar. 20
les Poissons 🗣 lay pwason

ARIES

Mar. 21 – Apr. 20
le Bélier 🗣 luh belly-er

TAURUS

Apr. 21 – May 21
le Taureau 🗣 luh tor-oh

GEMINI

May 22 – June 21
les Gémeaux 🗣 lay jem-oh

CANCER

June 22 – July 23
le Cancer 🗣 luh cancer

LEO

July 24 – Aug. 23
le Lion 🗣 luh lee-on

VIRGO

Aug. 24 – Sep. 23
la Vierge 🗣 la vee-er]

LIBRA

Sep. 24 – Oct. 23
la Balance 🗣 la ba-lons

SCORPIO

Oct. 24 – Nov. 22
le Scorpion 🗣 luh scorpion

SAGITTARIUS

Nov. 23 – Dec. 21
le Sagittaire 🗣 luh sajitair

CAPRICORN

Dec. 22 – Jan. 20
le Capricorne 🗣 luh capricorn

13

14

football le foot
👄 luh foot

rollerblading
le roller
👄 luh roller

music
la musique
👄 la mew-zeek

electronic games
les jeux électroniques
👄 lay juh ay-lek-tro-neek

tv
la télé
👄 la taylay

comics
la BD
👄 la bay-day

teddy bears
les nounours
👄 lay noonoor

school
l'école
👄 lay-kol

spiders les araignées
👄 layz aran-nyay

15

What's your favourite ...?
Quel est ton/ta ... préféré(e)?
👄 kel ay ton/tah ... preh-fairay

group
(ton) groupe
👄 (ton) groop

colour
(ta) couleur
👄 (tah) koo-luh

Page 69

game
(ton) jeu
👄 (ton) juh

snack
(ton) goûter
👄 (ton) gootay

ring tone
(ta) sonnerie
👄 (tah) soneree

animal
(ton) animal
👄 (ton) a-nee-mal

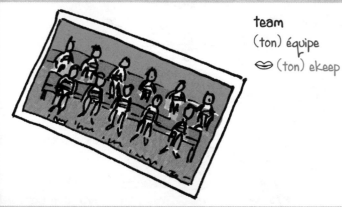

team
(ton) équipe
👄 (ton) ekeep

Talk about your pets

He's hungry
Il a faim
👄 eel ah fam

She's sleeping
Elle fait dodo 👄 el fay dodo

Can I stroke your dog?
Je peux caresser ton chien?
👄 juh puh karessay ton shyan

Do you have any pets?
T'as des animaux de compagnie?
👄 tah dayz ani-moh duh kopanyee

18

dog
le chien
👄 luh shee-an

cat
le chat
👄 luh sha

guinea pig
le cochon d'Inde
👄 luh ko-shon d'and

snake
le serpent
👄 luh sir-pon

hamster
le hamster
👄 luh amster

parakeet
la perruche
👄 la peroosh

My little doggy goes *oua-oua-oua!*

A French doggy (that's "toutou" in baby language) doesn't say "woof, woof", it says *"oua, oua"* (*waa-waa*). A French sheep says *"bêê, bêê!"* (*bear-bear*) and a cluck-cluck in French chicken-speak is *"cot-cot"* (*ko-ko*). But cats do say "miaow" whether they're speaking French or English!

19

Talk about school (if you can stand it)

geography
la géo
👄 la jay-o

PE
la gym
👄 la jeem

art
le dessin
👄 luh dessa

French
le français
👄 luh fron-say

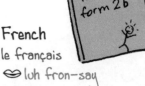

maths
les maths
👄 lay mat

English
l'anglais
👄 lon-glay

music
la musique
👄 la mew-zeek

English
m.smith
I love Sandra
x ❤ x

science
les sciences
👄 lay see-yons

history
l'histoire
👄 lis-twar

21

IT
l'informatique
👄 lanfor-mateek

Way unfair!

French children have very long vacation breaks: 9 weeks in the summer and another 6–7 weeks throughout the rest of the year. But before you turn green with envy, you might not like the mounds of "**devoirs de vacances**" (*duh-vwa duh vacans*), that's "vacation homework!" And if you fail your exams, the teachers could make you repeat the whole year with your little sister!

Talk about your phone

That's ancient
Il est super vieux!
👄 eel ay super vyuh

I've run out of credit
J'ai plus de forfait
👄 jay ploo duh forfay

What's your mobile like?
Il est comment ton portable?
👄 eel ay komon ton portabluh

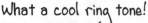

Lucky!
Trop de chance!
👄 troh duh shons

What a cool ring tone!
Elle est géniale ta sonnerie!
👄 el ay jenyal ta soneree

23

Gossip

Can you keep a secret?

Tu peux garder un secret?

👄 too puh garday uh sekray

Do you have a boyfriend (a girlfriend)?

T'as un petit ami (une petite amie)?

👄 tah uh pteet amee (oon pteet amee)

An OK guy/An OK girl

Un mec sympa/Une fille sympa

👄 uh mek sampa/oon fee sampa

What a bossy-boots!

Quel commandant!

👄 kel comon-don

He/She's nutty!

Il/Elle est dingue!

👄 eel/el ay dang

What a misery guts!

Quel râleur!

👄 kel rah-luh

You won't make many friends saying this!

Bog off!
Dégage!
👄 day-gaj

Shut up!
La ferme!
👄 la ferm

If you're fed up with someone, and you want to say something like "you silly …!" or "you stupid …!", you can start with **"espèce de"** (which actually means "piece of …") and add anything you like. What about …

Stupid banana!
Espèce de banane!
(espes duh banan)

or …

Silly sausage!
Espèce d'andouille!
(espes don-dooy)

Take your pick. It should do the trick. You could also try **"espèce d'idiot!"** *(espes dee-dyo)*. You don't need a translation here, do you?

25

You might have to say

Bother!
La vache!
👄 la vash

Rats!
Zut!
👄 zoot

"Did someone call me?"

la vache

That's not funny
C'est pas marrant
👄 say pah marron

That's plenty!
C'est bon!
👄 say bon

I'm fed up
J'en ai ras-le-bol
👄 jon nay ral-bol

26

Stop!
Arrête!
👄 aret

I want to go home!
Je veux rentrer chez moi
👄 juh vuh rentray
shay mwah

I don't care
Je m'en fiche
👄 juh mon feesh

At last!
C'est pas trop tôt!
👄 say pah tro toe

27

Saying goodbye

Here's my address
Voilà mon adresse
👄 vla mon adres

What's your address?
Tu m'donnes ton adresse?
👄 too mdon ton adres

Come to visit me
Viens chez moi
👄 vya shay mwa

How do you say goodbye to a skeleton?

Bone Voyage!

28

Have a good trip!
Bon voyage!
👄 bon vwoy-arj

Write to me soon
Écris-moi vite
👄 ekree mwa veet

Send me a text
Envois-moi un texto
👄 onvwa-mwa uh texto

Let's chat online
On chat sur internet
👄 on "chat" syur internet

Bye!
Au revoir!
👄 oh rev-wa

What's your email address?
C'est quoi ton e-mail?
👄 say kwa ton e-mail

⊃▢@3◇*☺ℛ.com

WANNA PLAY?

l'élastique
👄 lelasteek

le ping-pong
👄 luh "ping pong"

le baladeur
🗣 luh balad-er

W
A
N
N
A
P
L
A
Y
?

le portable
🗣 luh porta-bluh

le yo-yo
🗣 luh yo-yo

Do you want to play ...?
Tu veux jouer ...?
👄 too vuh joo-ay

... table football?
... au baby-foot?
👄 oh baby foot

... cards?
... aux cartes?
👄 oh kart

... on the computer?
... sur l'ordinateur?
👄 syur lordee-nater

... noughts and crosses?
... au morpion?
👄 oh more-pyon

Care for a game of **cat** or **leap sheep**?!

In France, playing tag is called playing "at cat"—**à chat** (*asha*). Whoever is "it" is the cat—**le chat** (*luh sha*). And you don't play "leap frog", you play "leap sheep"—**saute mouton** (*sote moo-ton*). Have you ever seen a sheep leaping?

Can my friend play too?
Mon copain peut jouer aussi?
👄 mo kopan puh jooway oh-see

I have to ask my parents
Il faut que je demande à mes vieux
👄 eel foh kuh juh daymon ah may vyuh

Make yourself heard

Who dares?

You're it!
Touché!
👄 tooshay

Race you!
On fait la course?
👄 on fay la koors?

I'm first
C'est moi le premier
👄 say mwa luh pre-myay

x

36

Electronic games

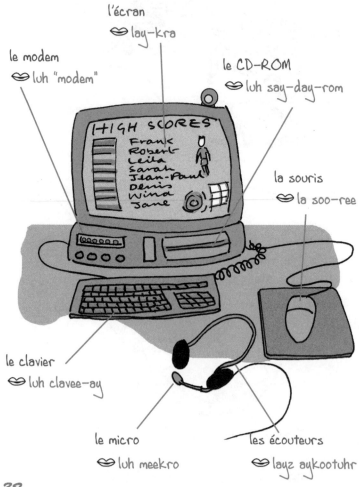

le modem
👄 luh "modem"

l'écran
👄 lay-kra

le CD-ROM
👄 luh say-day-rom

la souris
👄 la soo-ree

le clavier
👄 luh clavee-ay

le micro
👄 luh meekro

les écouteurs
👄 layz aykootuhr

38

39

It's virtual fun!

Do you have a webcam?
T'as une webcam?
👄 ta oon "webcam"

Send me a message.
Envois-moi un message.

How do i join?
Comment je m'inscris?

I'm not old enough.
Je suis pas assez grand.

I'm not allowed.
J'ai pas le droit.

I don't know who you are.
Je sais pas qui vous êtes.

40

my blog
mon blog
☻ mo "blog"

my contacts
mes contacts
☻ may kontakt

my photos
mes photos
☻ may foto

my videos
mes vidéos
☻ may vidayoh

my music ma musique
☻ ma mooseek

41

Non couch-potato activities!

tennis
le tennis
👄 luh "tennis"

trampolining
le trampoline
👄 luh "trampoline"

bowling
le bowling
👄 luh "bowling"

swimming
la natation
👄 la natasee-on

hockey
le hockey
👄 luh okee

gymnastics
la gymnastique
👄 la gymnasteek

ballet
le ballet
👄 luh ballay

basketball le basket
👄 luh basket

and, of course, we haven't forgotten *"le foot"* …

43

football

boots
les godasses
👄 lay godas

football strip
les affaires de foot
👄 layz afayr duh foot

ref
l'arbitre
👄 lar-beetruh

shin pads
les protèges-tibias
👄 lay protej-tibya

Well played!
Bien joué
👄 beeyah joo-way

Pass! Passe!
👄 pas

defender
le défenseur
👄 luh dayfonsur

attacker
l'attaquant
👄 latakon

Foul!
Coup-franc!
👄 koo fron

He pushed me!
Il m'a poussé!
👄 eel ma poo-say

Penalty!
Le penalty!
👄 luh paynalty

Goal!
Goal!
👄 just say it!

Keeping the others in line

Not like that!
Pas comme ça!
👄 pah kom sa

You cheat! Tricheur! (boys only)
Tricheuse! (girls only)
👄 tree-sher/tree-sherz

I'm not playing anymore
Je joue plus
👄 juh joo ploo

It's not fair!
C'est pas juste!
👄 say pah joost

Stop it!
Arrête!
👄 aret

47

Showing off

a handstand?
le poirier?
👄 luh pwa-riyay

Can you do ...
Tu sais faire ...
👄 too say fair

Look at me!
Regarde-moi!
👄 re-gard mwa

a cartwheel?
la roue?
👄 la roo

this?
ça?
👄 sa

48

Impress your French friends with this!

You can show off to your new French friends by practising this tongue twister:

Si ces six sausissons-ci sont six sous, ces six sausissons-ci sont très chers

see say see soseeson see son see soo, say see soseeson see son tray shair

(This means "If these six sausages cost six sous, these six sausages are very expensive.")

Then see if they can do as well with this English one:

"She sells seashells on the seashore, but the shells she sells aren't seashells, I'm sure."

For a rainy day

pack of cards
un jeu de cartes
👄 uh juh duh kart

my deal/your deal
à moi la donne/à toi la donne
👄 a mwa la don/a twa la don

king
le roi
👄 luh rwa

queen
la dame
👄 la dam

jack
le valet
👄 luh valay

joker
le joker
👄 luh jokair

trèfle
👄 tray-fluh

cœur
👄 kur

pique
👄 peek

carreau
👄 karo

50

snails
les escargots
👄 layz eskargo

mussels
les moules
👄 lay mool

a crème caramel
👄 la krem karamel

orange juice
le jus d'orange
👄 luh joo doronj

FEELING HUNGRY

Grub (la bouffe)

I'm starving
J'ai une faim de loup
👄 jay oon fam duh loo

That means "I have the hunger of a wolf!"

le loup

Please can I have ...
Donnez-moi, s'il vous plaît ...
👄 donay mwa, seel voo play

... a chocolate pastry
un pain au chocolat
👄 uh pan oh shokolah

... a croissant
un croissant
👄 uh kruh-son

... an apple turnover
un chausson aux pommes
👄 uh show-son oh pom

... a chocolate eclair
un éclair au chocolat
👄 uh eklair oh shokolah

... a bun with raisins
un pain aux raisins
👄 uh pan oh rayzan

Chocolate eclair? *"Miam, miam!"*
Snail pancake? *"Beurk!"*
If you're going to make food noises, you'll need to know how to do it properly in French!

"Yum, yum!" is out in French. You should

say *"Miam, miam!"* And "Yuk!" is *"Beurk"* (pronounced "burk"), but be careful not to let adults hear you say this!

55

... a baguette
une baguette
🗣 oon baget

... a pancake
une crêpe
🗣 oon krep

... a waffle
une gaufre
🗣 oon go-fruh

Did you know?

A lot of children have hot chocolate for breakfast in the morning and some of them will dip their bread or croissants or in it. It gets very soggy and Mum is sure not to like this!

I'm dying for a drink

Je meurs de soif
👄 juh mur duh swaf

I'd like ...
Je voudrais ...
👄 juh voodray

... a coke
... un coca
👄 uh koka

... an orange juice
... un jus d'orange
👄 uh joo doronj

... an apple juice
... un jus de pommes
👄 uh joo duh pom

57

... a lemonade
... une limonade
👄 oon leemonad

You can also have your lemonade with flavoured syrup —then it's called *"diabolo."* The most well-known is *"diabolo menthe"*, lemonade with mint syrup—hmmm!

... a syrup
un sirop
👄 uh seero

... a milkshake
... un milkshake
👄 uh meelkshek

You get your hot chocolate in a bowl (and that, at least, is a decent amount).

... a hot chocolate
... un chocolat
👄 uh shokolah

How did you like it?

That's lovely
C'est super-bon
👄 say soopair-bon

That's yummy
C'est géant
👄 say jay-on

I don't like that
J'aime pas ça
👄 jem pah sa

I'm stuffed
J'ai trop bouffé
👄 jay tro boofay

I can't eat that
Je mange pas ça
👄 juh monj pah sa

That's gross
C'est dégoûtant
👄 say day-gooton

59

A "crunchy man" sandwich, please.

You never thought you could crunch up a man in France and get away with it, did you? Well, in France a grilled ham-and-cheese sandwich is:

un croque-monsieur
👄 uh krok murs-yur

… that means a "crunchy man." There's also a "crunchy woman!"

un croque-madame
👄 uh krok ma-dam

… which is the same but with a fried egg on top.

Tales of snails

Did you know that snails have to be put in a bucket of salt water for three days to clean out their insides (don't ask!). After that they are baked in the oven in their shells and eaten with tons of garlic butter. And many French kids still love them!

Parties

French children often sing "Happy Birthday" in English when the candles are blown out on the cake. So you can practise singing the words with a French accent!

balloon la balle
👄 la bal

appee birzday too yoo!
appee birzday too yoo!

Can I have some more?
Je peux en avoir d'autre?
👄 juh puh avwah door-truh

party hat
le chapeau cotillon
👄 luh shapoh koteeyon

This is for you
C'est pour toi
👄 say poor twa

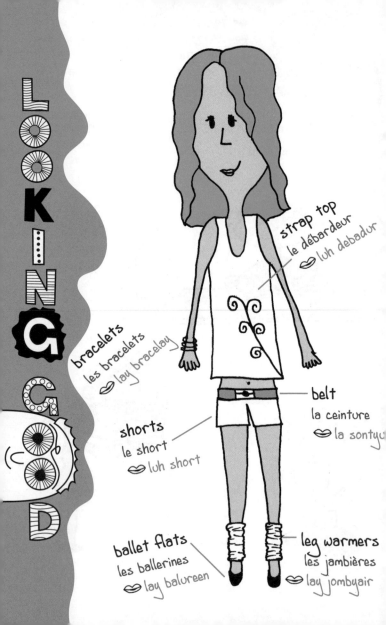

cap
la casquette
👄 la kasket

mp3
le Mp3
👄 luh em-
pay twa

hoodie
la cagoule
👄 la kagool

tattoo
le tatouage
👄 luh tattoo-arj

jeans
le jean
👄 luh jeen

trainers
les baskets
👄 lay basket

LOOKING GOOD

spotty à pois
👄 a pwa

flowery à fleurs
👄 a fler

frilly à frous-frous
👄 a froo froo

glittery à paillettes
👄 a pie-et

stripey à rayures
👄 a rayure

Clothes

jeans
le jean
👄 luh

sweatshirt
le sweat
👄 luh swet

T-shirt
le T-shirt
👄 luh "T-shirt"

football shirt
le maillot de foot
👄 luh mayo duh foot

trainers
les baskets
👄 lay basket

shoes
les chaussures
👄 lay show-soor

skirt
la jupe
👄 la joop

dress
la robe
👄 la rob

trousers
le pantalon
👄 luh panta-lon

Where's my trouser?!

The French don't wear "trouser**s**" or "jean**s**" – they wear only one of them: un pantalon *(uh pan-taloh)*; un jean *(uh jeen)*. Strange, could've sworn they had two legs!

67

Make it up!

lip gloss
le gloss
👄 luh gloss

nail varnish
le vernis à ongles
👄 luh vairnee a ongluh

glitter gel
le gel à paillettes
👄 luh jel a pie-yet

earrings
les boucles d'oreilles
👄 lay boo-kluh doray

eye shadow
le fard à paupières
👄 luh fardah po-pyair

I need a mirror
J'ai besoin d'un miroir
👄 jay buzwa duh mirwa

Can you lend me your straighteners?
Tu peux me prêter ton fer à lisser?
👄 too puh muh pretay ton fair a leezay

68

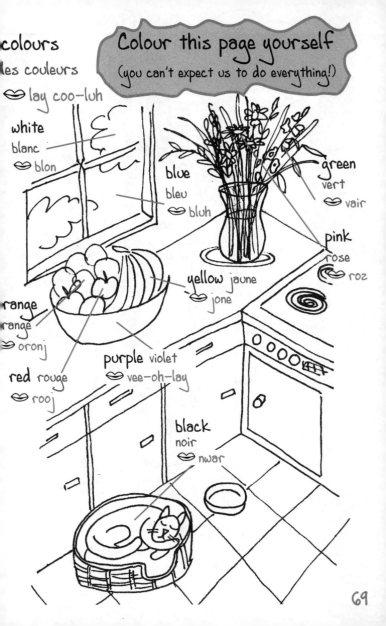

colours

les couleurs

🗣 lay coo-luh

Colour this page yourself
(you can't expect us to do everything!)

white
blanc
🗣 blon

blue
bleu
🗣 bluh

green
vert
🗣 vair

pink
rose
🗣 roz

yellow jaune
🗣 jone

orange
orange
🗣 oronj

purple violet
🗣 vee-oh-lay

red rouge
🗣 rooj

black
noir
🗣 nwar

69

What should we do?
Qu'est-ce qu'on fait?
😋 kesk on'fay

Can I come?
Je peux venir?
😋 juh puh vuneer

Where do you all hang out?
Où traînez-vous?
😋 oo trainay voo

That's mega!
C'est géant!
😋 say jay-on

I'm (not) allowed
J'ai (pas) le droit
😋 jay (pa) luh drwa

72

Let's go back On y retourne
👄 onny rutoorn

That gives me goose bumps (or "chicken flesh" in French!)
Ça m'donne la chair de poule
👄 sa mdon la shair duh pool

I'm bored to death
C'est mortel
👄 say mortell

HOUSE OF MIRRORS

That's funny
C'est marrant
👄 say maron

73

Beach babes

Can I borrow this?
Tu me prêtes ça?
☺ too muh pret sa

Let's hit the beach!
On va à la plage
☺ on va a la plarj

Is this your bucket?
C'est ton seau?
☺ say toh so

You can bury me
Tu peux m'enterrer
☺ too puh moterray

Stop throwing sand!
Arrête de jeter du sable!
☺ arret duh jetay dew sabluh

Watch out for my eyes!
Attention à mes yeux!
☺ attensee-on
a maiz yuh

74

sea
la mer
🔊 la mair

beach la plage
🔊 la plarj

sandcastle
le château de sable
🔊 luh shato duh sabluh

towel
la serviette
🔊 la sir-vee-et

bathing costume
le maillot
🔊 luh my-yo

bucket
le seau
🔊 luh so

spade la pelle
🔊 la pel

snorkel
le tuba
🔊 luh tew-ba

shells
les coquillages
🔊 lay kokeeyarj

How to get rid of your parents and eat lots of chocolate!

In France there are great beach clubs that organise all sorts of games as well as competitions (sandcastles, sports, etc.). The prizes are often given by large companies who make kids' stuff such as chocolate and toys. Insist on signing up!

75

It's going swimmingly!

How to make a splash in French!

PLOUF

Let's hit the swimming pool
On va à la piscine
👄 on va a la piseen

Can you swim (underwater)?
Tu sais nager (sous l'eau)?
👄 too say najay (soo lo)

Me too/I can't
Moi aussi/Moi pas
👄 mwa os-see/ mwa pa

Can you dive?
Tu sais plonger?
👄 too say plonjay

I'm getting changed
Je me change 👄 juh muh shanj

Can you do ...?
Tu sais faire ...?
👄 too say fair

backstroke
le dos crawlé
👄 luh doe krolay

butterfly
le papillon
👄 luh papeeyon

crawl
le crawl
👄 luh krol

breaststroke
la brasse 👄 la brass

slide
le toboggan
👄 luh tobogan

goggles
les lunettes de plongée
👄 lay loonet
duh plonjay

77

Do you know the way?
Tu connais le chemin?
👄 too konay luh shema

Pooper-scoopers on wheels!

You might see bright green-and-white motorcycles with funny vacuum cleaners on the side riding around town scooping up the dog poop. The people riding the bikes look like astronauts! (Well, you'd want protection too, wouldn't you?)

Let's ask
On va demander
👄 o va demonday

bus
le bus
👄 luh boos

Is it far?
C'est loin?
👄 say lwan

Are we allowed in here?
On a le droit d'entrer ici?
👄 on a luh drwa dentray eessee

car la bagnole
👄 la banyol

The "proper" French word for car is **"voiture"** (*vwat-yure*), but you'll look very uncool saying this. Stick to **"bagnole"** (*banyol*), or if the car is a wreck, try **"tacot"** (*taco*) for even more street cred: **"Quel tacot!"** (*kel tako*—"What an old banger!").

79

Park yourself here

swings la balançoire
🗣 la balonswar

climbing frame la cage à poules 🗣 la kaj ah pool

playground l'aire de jeu
🗣 lair duh juh

grass l'herbe
🗣 lairb

tree l'arbre
🗣 larbruh

slide
le toboggan
🗣 luh tobogan

80

park le parc 🗣 luh park

Can we play ball games?
On peut jouer au ballon?
👄 on puh jooway oh balon

roundabout
le tourniquet
👄 luh toornikay

sandpit
le bac à sable
👄 luh bakah sabluh

Can I have a go? Je peux essayer? 👄 juh puh esay-yay

Picnic (le pique-nique)

I hate wasps
Je déteste les guêpes
☞ juh daytest
lay gep

Move over!
Pousse-toi!
☞ poos twa

bread
le pain ☞ luh pan

Let's sit here
On s'assoie ici?
☞ on saswa eessee

ham le jambon
☞ luh jambon

napkin
la serviette
☞ la sir-vee-et

cheese
le fromage
☞ luh fromarj

yoghurt
le yaourt
☞ luh ya-oort

crisps
les chips
☞ lay sheep

drinks
les boissons
👄 lay bwason

knife
le couteau
👄 luh koo-toe

spoon
la cuillère
👄 la kwee-yeah

fork
la fourchette
👄 la four-shet

wasps
les guêpes
👄 lay gep

bees
les abeilles
👄 layz abay

bzzzz

ants
les fourmis
👄 lay foor-mee

83

Wake up, campers!

tent la tente
👄 la tont

tent peg
le piquet de tente
👄 luh peekay duh tont

camper van
le camping-car
👄 luh komping car

penknife
le couteau suisse
👄 luh kootoh swees

camping stove
le camping gaz
👄 luh komping gaz

sleeping bag le sac de couchage
👄 luh sak duh kooshaj

torch
la lampe de poche
👄 la lomp
duh posh

84

That tent's a palace!
Cette tente, c'est la classe!
👄 set tont, say la klas

campfire
le feu de camp
👄 luh fuh duh komp

I've lost my torch
J'ai paumé ma lampe de poche
👄 jay pomay ma lomp duh posh

These showers are gross
Ces douches sont crades
👄 say doosh son krad

Where does the rubbish go?
Où est-ce qu'on jette les ordures?
👄 oo eskon jet layz ordyur

All the fun of the fair

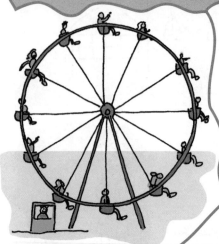

helter-skelter
le toboggan 🗨 luh tobogar

big wheel
la grande roue
🗨 la grond roo

house of mirrors
le palais des glaces
🗨 luh palay day glas

bumper cars
les autos tamponneuses
🗨 layz oto tomponerz

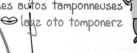

Let's try this
On essaie ça?
🗨 on essay sa

86

roundabout
le manège
🗣 luh manayj

It's (too) fast
Ça va (trop) vite
🗣 sa va (tro) veet

That's for babies
C'est pour les petits
🗣 say poor lay ptee

Do you get wet in here?
On sort mouillé d'ici?
🗣 on sor moo-yay deessee

I'm not going on my own
J'y vais pas tout seul
🗣 jee vay pa too surl

87

Disco nights

mirror ball
la boule multi-facettes
👄 la bool multee-faset

loudspeakers
les enceintes
👄 layz onsent

Can I request a song?
Je peux demander qu'on passe une chanson? 👄 juh puh dumonday kon pas oon shonso

The music is really lame
La musique est vraiment nulle
👄 la mooseek ay vraymon nool

spotlights
les spots
👄 lay spot

DJ le DJ
👄 luh "DJ"

mixing desk la table de mixage 👄 la tabluh duh meeksarj

How old do I need to be?

Quel âge il faut avoir?

👄 kel aj eel foh avwah

dance floor

la piste de danse

👄 la peest duh dons

Let's dance!

On danse!

👄 on dons

I love this song!

J'adore cette chanson!

👄 jadoor set shonso

POCKET MONEY

sweets
les bonbons
🖙 lay bonbon

les T-shirts
🖙 lay "T-shirt"

toys les jouets
🖙 lay joo-ay

le vendeur
🖙 luh von-du

books
les livres
👄 lay lee-vruh

le mobile
👄 luh mobeel

les crayons
👄 lay crayon
Watch out! This means *pencils* NOT crayons!

What does that sign say?

pâtisserie
cake shop
👄 pateesree

boucherie
butcher shop
👄 booshree

boulangerie
bakery
👄 boolonjree

confiserie
sweet shop
👄 konfeesree

papeterie
stationary shop
👄 paptree

épicerie
grocer
👄 aypeesree

boutique de vêtements
clothes shop
👄 booteek duh vetmon

92

Do you have some cash?
T'as des sous?
🗣 tah day soo

I'm broke
Je suis fauché
🗣 juh swee foshay

I'm loaded
J'ai plein d'sous
🗣 jay pla dsoo

Here you go
Voilà
🗣 vla

That's a weird shop!
Quel magasin bizarre!
🗣 kel maguzah beezar

That's a bargain C'est pas cher
🗣 say pa shair

It's a rip-off
C'est du vol
🗣 say dew vol

93

Sweet heaven!

I love this shop
J'adore cette boutique
👄 jadore set booteek

Let's get some sweets
On va acheter des bonbons
👄 on va ashtay day bonbon

Let's get some ice-cream
On va acheter une glace
👄 on va ashtay oon glas

lollipops
des sucettes
👄 day sooset

a bar of chocolate
une tablette de chocolat
👄 oon tablet duh shokola

chewing gum
chewing gum
👄 just say it, will you!

If you really want to look French and end up with lots of fillings, ask for:

des Carambars™ (day caram-bar)

medium-hard toffee-bars, also available in all sorts of fruity flavours; popular for the desperately silly jokes to be found inside the wrappings

des Malabars™ (day malabar)

bubble-gum, also popular for the tattoos provided with them

des nounours en chocolat (day noonoors on shokola)

teddy-shaped marshmallow-type sweets in chocolate coating

des frites (day freet)

fruity gums, slightly fizzy, shaped like chips

des Mini Berlingot™ (day mini berlingo)

sugary creamy stuff sold in small squishy packets — a bit like a small version of the "lunchbox" yoghurts

des Dragibus™ (day drajibus)

multicoloured licorice jelly beans

Other things you could buy
(that won't ruin your teeth!)

What are you getting?
Qu'est-ce tu prends?
👄 keska too pron

That toy, please
Ce jouet là, s'il vous plaît
👄 suh joo-ay la, seel voo pla

Two postcards, please
Deux cartes postales,
s'il vous plaît
👄 duh kart
post-tal,
seel voo play

This is rubbish
C'est nul
👄 say nool

This is cool
C'est cool
👄 say kool

I'm getting ...

J'achète ... 😊 jashait

... a pen un stylo
😊 uh stee-lo

... stamps
des timbres
😊 day timbruh

... felt-tip pens
des feutres
😊 day fer-truh

... coloured pencils
des crayons de couleur
😊 day krayon duh koolur

... a key ring
un porte-clés
😊 uh port klay

... comics
des BD
😊 day bay day

97

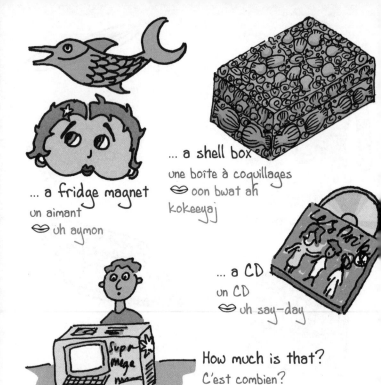

... a shell box
une boîte à coquillages
👄 oon bwat ah kokeeyaj

... a fridge magnet
un aimant
👄 uh aymon

... a CD
un CD
👄 uh say-day

How much is that?
C'est combien?
👄 say kombee-yah

For many years France's favourite comics have been Astérix and Tintin. They have both been translated into English, as well as into many other languages. Today children also like to read:

Tom Tom et Nana
Boule et Bill
Natacha
Gaston Lagaffe

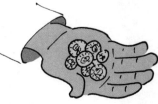

Money talks

How much pocket money do you get?

T'as combien d'argent de poche?

💬 tah komee-yah darjon duh posh

I only have this much

J'ai seulement ça

💬 jay sulmo sah

Can you lend me ten euros?

Tu peux me prêter dix euros

💬 too puh muh pretay dee yooro

No way!

Pas question!

💬 pa kes-tyo

Money talk

French money is the **euro** (pronounced *ew-roh*).
A euro is divided into 100 **centimes** (*senteem*).
Coins: 1, 2, 5, 10, 20, 50 **centimes**

      1, 2 **euros**

Notes: 5, 10, 20, 50, 100 **euros**

Make sure you know how much you are spending before you blow all your pocket money at once!

GROWN UP TALK

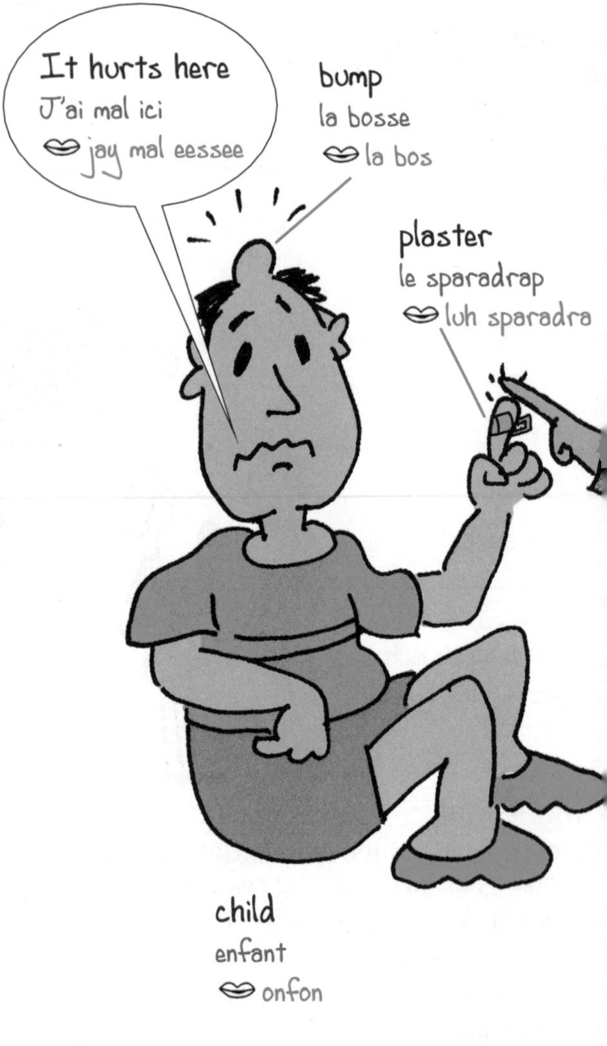

Help!

Something has dropped/broken
Quelque chose est tombé/cassé
👄 kel-kuh shose ay tombay/kassay

Please
S'il vous plaît
👄 seel voo play

Can you help me?
Vous pouvez m'aider?
👄 voo poovay mayday

Where's the post box?
Où est la boîte aux lettres?
👄 oo ay la bwat oh lettruh

Where are the toilets?
Où sont les toilettes?
👄 oo son lay twalet

102

I can't manage it
Je n'y arrive pas
👄 juh nee arreev pah

Could you pass me that?
Vous pouvez me passer ça?
👄 voo poovay muh passay sa

What time is it?
Quelle heure il est?
👄 kel ur eelay

Come and see
Venez voir
👄 venay vwar

May I look at your watch?
Je peux voir sur votre montre?
👄 juh puh vwar syur votruh montruh

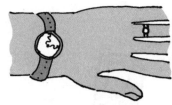

Lost for words

... **my ticket**
mon billet
👄 mo beeyay

I've lost ...
J'ai perdu ...
👄 jay perdew

... **my mobile**
mon portable
👄 mo portabluh

... **my parents**
mes parents
👄 may paron

... **my shoes**
mes chaussures
👄 may sho-syur

... **my money** mon argent
👄 mo arjon

... **my sweater**
mon pull
👄 mo pool

... **my watch**
ma montre
👄 ma montruh

... **my jacket** ma veste
👄 ma vest

Adults only!

Show this page to adults who can't seem to make themselves clear (it happens). They will point to a phrase, you read what they mean, and you should all understand each other perfectly.

Ne t'en fais pas
Don't worry

Assieds-toi ici
Sit down here

Quel est ton nom et ton prénom?
What's your name and surname?

Quel âge as-tu?
How old are you?

D'où viens-tu?
Where are you from?

Où habites-tu?
Where are you staying?

Où est-ce que tu as mal?
Where does it hurt?

Est-ce que tu es allergique à quelque chose?
Are you allergic to anything?

C'est interdit
It's forbidden

Tu dois être accompagné d'un adulte
You have to have an adult with you

Je vais chercher quelqu'un qui parle anglais
I'll get someone who speaks English

EXTRA STUFF

weather
le temps
👄 luh toh

numbers les nombres 👄 lay nom

time
l'heure
lur

EXTRA STUFF

There was an English cat called "one, two, three" and a French cat called "un, deux, trois" standing waiting to cross a river. Both were afraid of water, so the English cat suggested that they race across to make it more fun. Who won?

Answer: "One, two, three" because "un, deux, trois" CAT SANK!

un	un	
deux	duh	
trois	twa	
quatre	katruh	
cinq	sank	
six	sees	

110

sept   👄 set

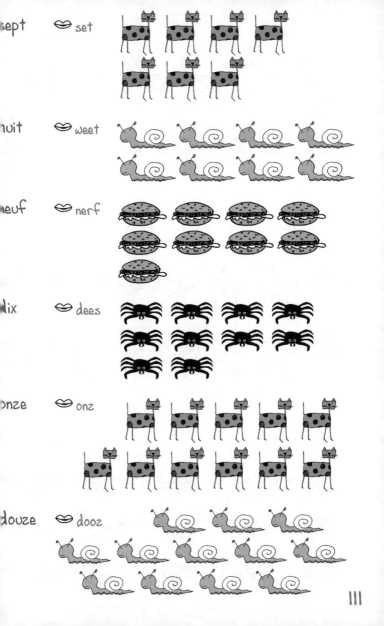

huit   👄 weet

neuf   👄 nerf

dix   👄 dees

onze   👄 onz

douze   👄 dooz

treize 👄 trez

quatorze 👄 catorz

quinze 👄 kanz

16 seize	*sez*	19 dix-neuf	*dees-nerf*
17 dix-sept	*dees-set*	20 vingt	*van*
18 dix-huit	*dees-weet*		

I f you want to say "twenty-two", "sixty-five", and so on, you can just put the two numbers together like you do in English:

22 **vingt-deux**   *van duh*

65 **soixante cinq** *swasont sank*

This works except if you're saying "twenty-one", "sixty-one", and so on. Then you need to add the word for "and" (**et**) in the middle:

21 **vingt et un**   *vant eh un*

61 **soixante et un** *swasont eh un*

30 trente	*tront*
40 quarante	*karont*
50 cinquante	*sankont*
60 soixante	*swasont*
70 soixante-dix	*swasont dees*
80 quatre-vingts	*katruh van*
90 quatre-vingt-dix	*katruh van dees*
100 cent	*sonn*

The French must be really big on sums! Everything's fine until you reach 70. Instead of saying "seventy," they say "sixty-ten" (*soixante-dix*) and keep counting like this until they reach 80. So 72 is "sixty-twelve" (*soixante douze*), 78 is "sixty-eighteen" (*soixante dix-huit*), and so on.

Just so it doesn't get too easy, for 80 they say "4 twenties!" And to really make your brain ache they continue counting like this until a hundred. So 90 is "4 twenties 10" (*quatre-vingt-dix*), 95 is "4 twenties fifteen" (*quatre-vingt-quinze*) … you remembered your calculator, didn't you??

1,000 mille *meel*

a million *un million uh mil-yo*

billions and billions! *des milliards de milliards!*
day meelyar duh meelyar

March	mars	*mars*
April	avril	*avreel*
May	mai	*meh*

June	juin	*joo-wah*
July	juillet	*joowee-eh*
August	août	*oot*

September	septembre	*septombruh*
October	octobre	*octobruh*
November	novembre	*novombruh*

December	décembre	*desombruh*
January	janvier	*jonvee-eh*
February	février	*fevree-eh*

printemps *prantom*

SPRING

été *eteh*

SUMMER

automne *awtom*

AUTUMN

hiver *eever*

WINTER

Monday	lundi	*lundee*
Tuesday	mardi	*mardee*
Wednesday	mercredi	*mecredee*
Thursday	jeudi	*jurdee*
Friday	vendredi	*vendredee*
Saturday	samedi	*samdee*
Sunday	dimanche	*deemonsh*

By the way, French kids don't usually have school on Wednesdays, but they have to go on Saturday mornings. Still—that's half a day less than you!

Good times

It's ...
Il est ...
👄 eel ay

(one) o'clock
(une) heure
👄 (oon) ur

quarter past (two)
(deux heures) et quart
👄 (duh zur) ay kar

quarter to (four)
(quatre heures) moins le quart
👄 (katr ur) mwan luh kar

half past (three)
(trois heures) et demie
👄 (twa zur) ay demee

five past (ten)
(dix heures) cinq
👄 dees ur sank

twenty past (eleven)
(onze heures) vingt
👄 onz ur van

ten to (four)
(quatre heures) moins dix
👄 (katr ur) mwan dees

twenty to (six)
(six heures) moins vingt
👄 (sees ur) mwan van

121

morning
matin
🗣 ma–tah

midday
midi
🗣 meedee

afternoon
après–midi
🗣 apray meedee

midnight
minuit
🗣 meenwee

evening soir
🗣 swar

122

now maintenant
👄 mantenon

night
nuit
👄 nwee

today
aujourd'hui
👄 oh jordwee

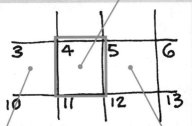

| 3 | 4 | 5 | 6 |
| 10 | 11 | 12 | 13 |

yesterday
hier
👄 ee-air

tomorrow
demain
👄 duh-man

123

Weather wise

Can we go out?
On peut sortir?
👄 on puh sorteer

It's hot
Il fait chaud
👄 eel fay show

It's cold
Il fait froid
👄 eel fay frwa

It's horrible
Il fait mauvais
👄 eel fay movay

It's raining ropes!

In French it doesn't rain "cats and dogs," it rains "ropes!" That's what they say when it's raining really heavily:

Il pleut des cordes
eel pluh day kord

124

It's windy
Il fait du vent
👄 eel fay dew von

It's sunny
Il fait du soleil
👄 eel fay dew solay

It's raining
Il pleut
👄 eel pluh

It's snowing
Il neige
👄 eel nej

I'm soaked
Je me suis fait tremper
👄 juh muswee fay trompay

It's nice Il fait beau
👄 eel fay bow

125

Signs of life

Taille Minimum
Minimum Height

Eteindre les téléphones

Turn off your telephone

Entrée Interdite

No Entry

Interdit aux moins de dix-huit ans

Under 18s not allowed